CW00729500

DANCING ATTENDANCE

DANCING ATTENDANCE
by Lucy Gannon

Warner Chappell Plays

LONDON

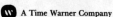 A Time Warner Company

First published 1990
by Warner Chappell Plays Ltd.,
129 Park Street, London W1Y 3FA

© Copyright Lucy Gannon, 1990

ISBN 0 85676 151 6

This play is protected by Copyright. According to Copyright Law, no public performance or reading of a protected play or part of that play may be given without prior authorization from Warner Chappell Plays Ltd., as agent for the Copyright Owners.

From time to time it is necessary to restrict or even withdraw the rights of certain plays. It is therefore essential to check with us before making a commitment to produce a play.

NO PERFORMANCE MAY BE GIVEN WITHOUT A LICENCE

AMATEUR PRODUCTIONS
Royalties are due at least fourteen days prior to the first performance. Licences will be issued upon receipt of remittances accompanied by the following details.

Name of Licensee
Play Title
Place of Performance
Dates and Number of Performances
Audience Capacity
Ticket Prices

PROFESSIONAL PRODUCTIONS
All enquiries regarding professional rights (other than first class rights) should be addressed to Warner Chappell Plays Ltd. Enquiries concerning all other rights should be addressed to Lemon, Unna and Durbridge Ltd., 24 Pottery Lane, Holland Park, London W11 4LZ.

OVERSEAS PRODUCTIONS
Applications for productions overseas should be addressed to our local authorized agents. Further details available from Warner Chappell Plays, London.

CONDITIONS OF SALE
This book is sold subject to the condition that it shall not by way of trade or otherwise be re-sold, hired out, circulated or distributed without prior consent of the Publisher. Reproduction of the text either in whole or in part and by any means is strictly forbidden.

Typeset and printed by Commercial Colour Press, London E7.

DANCING ATTENDANCE was first presented at the Bush Theatre, London on 9th November, 1990, with the following cast:

JACK SLANEY	Barry Foster
ZITA SLANEY	Cherith Mellor
REG DALTON	David Beames

Directed by Stuart Burge
Designed by Annie Smart
Lighting Designed by Tina MacHugh

A Bush Theatre Production.

Cast

JACK SLANEY   Not more than sixty years old. He's powerfully built but a series of strokes has left him unable to walk and with paralysis and rigidity in his right arm. He has a strong physical presence.

ZITA SLANEY   Not more than forty years old.

REG DALTON   In his thirties, certainly not older than Zita. Dressed cheaply.

A set of door frames around a small living area – one to the kitchen, one to the outside, one to SLANEY's room and another from that to the bathroom.

We should be able to see SLANEY as he lies in his bedroom during the second act.

The living area suggested by cosy colours, an armchair and a settee.

ACT ONE
Scene One

SLANEY *is sitting in an armchair.* ZITA *in kitchen putting shopping away.*

SLANEY	Are we eating tonight, or what?
ZITA	(*off*) Slaney!
SLANEY	Just wondering.
ZITA	Have an apple.
SLANEY	What a good idea! Apple! Apple! Come to Slaney! (*Fingers in the corners of his mouth, he whistles.*) App – le! Come to Sla-ney!
ZITA	(*striding in, throwing an apple onto his lap*) Kid! (*She strides off again.*)
SLANEY	What are you doing?
ZITA	The shopping doesn't unpack itself.
SLANEY	(*to himself*) Never said it did. (*Louder.*) I never said it did. (SLANEY *holds the apple up as if he was a small inquisitive animal examining it.*) Yum yum. Crunch! Spit. Slurp. (*Louder.*) Juicy! Juicy! Juicy!
ZITA	Yes, well, just make sure you chew it properly.
SLANEY	Mmmmmmm. Gobble, gobble, grub and grobble. Nibble. twizzle, gnaw and fizzle. Down the red brick road, core and skin and pips and chokey bits and all.
ZITA	Are you trying to tell me that you'd like it peeled?
SLANEY	Oh, don't worry. All grist to the mill. (*Takes a huge bite.*) You will remember to hook your index finger down the back of my gullet, won't you?
ZITA	(*going away again*) I shouldn't bank on it.

SLANEY	(*trying to wipe the juice that runs down his chin*) Nothing like a Cox's Orange Pipp– (*Starts to cough. She comes back, reluctant to interfere. He bends over his hand, his face grows red, his shoulders heave, he gasps.*)
ZITA	Slaney! (*She runs to him but as she touches his shoulder he uncoils magically, beaming at her, holding up the apple victoriously.*)
SLANEY	Gotcher!
ZITA	You stupid old bugger! (*She swipes the apple back and goes back into the kitchen, angrily.*)
SLANEY	I'm not an apple eater, me. Are we having proper food tonight?
ZITA	Didn't the SS give you any tea?
SLANEY	A few biscuits. Not proper tea.
ZITA	More than I had.
SLANEY	You know I don't like biscuits. Can't remember the last time I actually ate a biscuit. (*He brings a packet of biscuits out of somewhere in his chair, takes one out, nibbles it delightedly.*) I'm not a biscuit eater, me. (*Again addressing ZITA.*) Your late mother used to make beautiful biscuits. Great trays of golden circles. Soft from the oven and crisp little wafers ten minutes later. Anyway, Mrs Wilson is not a proper SS. She doesn't know how to read the headlines. 'Peer nods off during debate' gets the same breathless input as 'Shock! Horror! Sexy goings on at Number Ten!'
ZITA	She's a nice little woman. And stop calling Mum 'my late mother'.
SLANEY	'Snooker Ace breaks up love nest' as deeply regretted as '326 Killed in Air Smash'.
ZITA	(*returning*) Do you want the commode before I start the food?

SLANEY	Charming pairing of ideas there.
ZITA	Do you?
SLANEY	What?
ZITA	Want the bloody lavatory?
SLANEY	Want the bloody lavatory to do what?
ZITA	(*exasperation*) Do you want to empty your bowels or vacate your bloody bladder?
SLANEY	No!
	(*There is a moment's silence.*)
	What sort of a day did you have?
ZITA	A Tuesday.
SLANEY	See ? See ? I try to be nice ...
ZITA	(*pouring herself a whisky, and sloshing a half tumbler of it for him*) Why have you got Mrs Wilson reading to you, anyway? It's your arm that's dodgy, not your eyes.
SLANEY	She gets thirty quid a week. And I'm educating her as we go along. Since she's been working here she's become a mature student.
ZITA	Mature as in 'one foot in the grave' I should think.
SLANEY	She's hardly overworked. Coffee at eleven, a sandwich for lunch and a cup of tea at three. Hardly toiling in the mines with no clothes on, is it?
ZITA	(*muttering*) Give me the choice.
SLANEY	(*frighteningly, explosively angry*) It's yours. No one's asking you to stay. Go on. Sod off out of it!
ZITA	(*after a pause*) Don't be silly, Slaney. You know I couldn't. Wouldn't want to.
SLANEY	(*quieter*) No. I was forgetting. It's your house.

ZITA   Do you want another drink?

(*He holds the glass out to her, his eyes filled with tears. She refills it, and gives the glass back to him.*)

ZITA   Our home. Well, that's the row for today out of the way.

SLANEY   Sit with me. Just for a minute. Forget the food. Please.

ZITA   OK. What's wrong with Mrs Wilson? Tell me.

SLANEY   Oh, I don't know, Zita. I just ... It isn't fair, what I'm doing to you.

ZITA   What?

SLANEY   Saving everything up for you. My moans, my groans, my bad tempers. My shit.

ZITA   Slaney ...

SLANEY   I do, you know.

ZITA   Don't be silly ...

SLANEY   I do! Her and her sister holiday in Bournemouth. Their one ambition used to be to get on 'Sale Of The Century'. Only, it's come off now, Sale of the Century. Such a nice man, Nicholas Parsons. How can I shit with her in the next room? Unless it was Tea Rose scented. And when I was in bed with 'flu – imagine if I'd got took short then! She'd want it surrounded by Royal Doulton flowers on a mother of pearl base.

ZITA   We could get it to pass out of the room on a conveyor belt, with a cuddly toy.

SLANEY   That was Bruce Forsyth. I suppose we could put concealed lighting in the bedpan, those optic fibre things.

ZITA   So that it changed colour as she took it to the lavatory?

SLANEY   From khaki to a restful green –

ZITA	And right through the blues to a baby pink–
SLANEY	And as she flushed it away the loo could play a tune –
ZITA	"We'll meet again ... "
SLANEY	Or "I do love to be beside the seaside ... " (*They are quiet for a moment.*) And so, because she wears pale pink and looks like my old Mum, I save my shit for you. (ZITA *starts to chuckle.*) What? (*He laughs too.*) What?
ZITA	Nothing. Well. Reminds me of an Andy Capp cartoon, ages ago. "Course I loves you. I smokes your fags, don't I?"
	(*They look at each other and the laughter grows, aided by the whisky.*)
ZITA	Better get some food, eh?
SLANEY	I love to hear you laugh. You should laugh more often! Oh, Christ, Zita, anyone looking at us now would think you were my missus.
ZITA	Thanks.
SLANEY	I want you to be like you were. Another six months at this rate and you'll be another ruddy Slaney sitter in a felt hat and a – look at you, for Christ's sake, you look forty –
ZITA	I am forty, Slaney!
SLANEY	And is it any wonder when you spend all the hours God gives you looking after a horrible old man – (*He flaps his hands helplessly, near to tears.*) Who cries easily, and shouts easily and –
ZITA	You need a good meal inside you, that's what you need. (*Goes into kitchen.*)
SLANEY	When did you decide to be forty? I can see you when you were a little girl in a pixie hat, laughing and rosey cheeked on the swings.

(*Noises are heard from the kitchen, off.*) I
imagined you then, grown up, and I pictured
us walking through the park together, arm in
arm, a distinguished old man and his
beautiful, successful daughter. And look at us
now. (*Pause.*) And I've sacked that old fart.
(*The noises off stop for a second, and then
continue.*) I told her to bugger off and never
darken our door again. Told her she was a
crabby, whining old bitch. Told her to stuff
her knitting where the joins would never
show. Actually. And stop crashing around in
there. The bloody floor's shaking!

(ZITA *strides in.*)

SLANEY　　(*changing tack, flamboyant*) There's are other
semi-senile Slaney sitters. (ZITA *folds her arms
and glares at him.*) Christ, there's something
primeval about a woman with her arms
folded. Terrifying.

(*He tries another tack, cajoling, playful.*)

No, I was very polite, but I did, in effect, tell
her to impale herself, right way up, on her
umbrella – telescopic, 99p at the market, not
a patch on her old one but then, for that
price, who can grumble? Left her good one
on the bus last Christmas, and people don't
hand things in like they did.

ZITA　　I walked across the green on my way home. I
met Mrs Wilson.

SLANEY　　In floods of tears, I suppose? Blaming
herself?

ZITA　　She said you'd been very good. So for one
bloody night pack in all the silly, silly bloody
games, the daily 'Call My Bluff' of life at The
Slaney's.

SLANEY　　I think that I am going mad. I think that my
personality has run its course and is now going
to seed, reaching wildly towards the light, like
an old brussels sprout plant. Scrawny,
yellowing and windblown.

My life is words and temper. I'm sitting on a
packet of biscuits. Know that? No? Well, I
am. Nicked them off the tray at tea time.
One up on the granny. One up on you.
Proof that I'm not a part of you.
Not a part of any bloody Slaney sitter. Not
her ticket to thirty quid a week. Not just that.
Do you know what she talks about all day?
Do you? (*Cruel mimic.*) Our Nigel came round
last night, with his wife, well, she's not his
wife, but what else can you call her? Never
think of that, do they, when they do away
with marrying. I knew they'd come of a
purpose. And we were that pleased when
they told us. Mind you, one look at her face
said everything. Well, it does, doesn't it?
But there, I acted surprised, you know.
I never like knitting pink or blue.
I mean, you never can tell, can you? No
matter what their scan things say, you never
can be sure. One little leg bent up and it's a
whole pile of baby gros wasted So, I say stick
to lemon, I do. What do you say? (*Yelling.*) I
say that I am Jack Slaney and I don't care if
you dress the snotty nosed little bastard in
sky blue pink with ruddy great purple
patches.

(ZITA *goes to comfort him. He pats her arm, speaks
more normally.*)

I really do think, Zita, that I am going mad.

ZITA   (*adopts a bantering tone, begins to massage his
              neck*) What you need is a good hot meal and
              an early night, my boy.

SLANEY   Oh, God, won't you listen to me? Zita,
              I ... am ... going ... mad.

ZITA   Well, then, can I come with you?

SLANEY   Zita ... (*Asking her to be honest, watching her
              face.*)

ZITA	(*making a game of it*) If that's where you're going then I want to come with you.
SLANEY	(*deflated*) It may be very boring.
ZITA	With you there? Never.
SLANEY	(*forcing himself to play along*) Grown up, then. Long speeches. That sort of thing.
ZITA	I'll bring a colouring book.
SLANEY	And you mustn't interrupt.
ZITA	I won't.
SLANEY	Or fidget.
ZITA	Let me come.
SLANEY	W .. e .. ll.
ZITA	Please?
SLANEY	Oh, alright. Spoilt brat. (*There are a few moments of silence while* ZITA *massages his neck.*)
ZITA	You're getting heavier. Know that? Look at the muscles on your neck. Brutish. I'm sure it hasn't always been like that.
SLANEY	It's the only bit of me that ever hurts.
ZITA	Poor neck. Pull yourself up while I do your back. Masseurs must be the most relaxed people in the world. Small circles, smooth movement, skin on skin. I signed the authorisation for two new word processors today. Linked into the computer system. Marketing and sales. It took me ten minutes, standing in the window, deep breathing, before I could bring myself to. Two and a half thousand pounds. Silly. And of course all the five-year 'do' is falling to me. And now they've decided that the meadow by the warehouse is too muddy for the marquee. I wish I'd never thought of it. No, I don't. But they seem to think that it was my idea so it can stay my idea.

Or perhaps it's because I'm a woman. I don't know. They want smoked salmon, champers, the lot. Outside caterers of course, but still there's a lot to be done ...
Bit different from the old works' 'do's, isn't it?
Five years! It doesn't seem that long. Slaney Printing plc.
Remember how worried you were about it? Remember when you went down to the solicitor's and signed all the papers? How –

SLANEY   That bit's sore.

ZITA   What?

SLANEY   I said, dammit, that bit's sore.

ZITA   Oh, sorry. (*Pause.*) They're all looking forward to seeing you. You'll not be short of pushers.

          (*There is a silence.*)

          Well, what have you been doing with yourself?

SLANEY   Raping, pillaging, looting. Usual stuff.

ZITA   On the shoulder blades. Golden skin. A smattering of freckles. There. Does that feel better?

SLANEY   (*energetically turning her tenderness away*) I remembered the book I wanted. Smith's I expect. Wrote it down, on my pad. John Mortimer. Do you mind?

ZITA   (*drawing his shirt up to his neck again, normal*) No. I don't mind. Well. Omlette, is it?

SLANEY   I fancy steak.

ZITA   I haven't got any steak.

SLANEY   Omlette, then.

ZITA   Sorry.

SLANEY   No. Omlette's fine. I like omlette.

Scene Two

When the lights rise again it is the next evening. During this scene
SLANEY *and* ZITA *gradually grow slightly drunk, slightly more*
belligerent than their norm.

SLANEY *sits alone, waiting for* ZITA *nervously. He hears her coming*
in and makes a visible effort to brighten up. ZITA *enters with one*
smallish carrier bag of shopping, brisk and cheerful.

SLANEY	Here she is!
ZITA	Here I am! (*Goes to him and pecks his cheek.*) Alright?
SLANEY	Wonderful. Good day?
ZITA	So so. (*She walks past him, taking her coat off as if to hang it up.*) Flaming auditors. Drive you scatty. Can't find any damn thing. Need spoon feeding, this year's lot do. (*Looking at him, curious.*) What's wrong?
SLANEY	Nothing. Well, I've got a surprise for you.
ZITA	A surprise? Really?
SLANEY	Get us a drink and I'll tell you.
ZITA	(*suspicious*) What is it?
SLANEY	Alcoholic poisoning first, please. (ZITA *goes and pours drinks.*)
ZITA	Not another Slaney carry-on, is it? (SLANEY *pulls a face behind her back.*)
SLANEY	I'm going to turn that into a sampler. Red white and blue cross stitch on an ecru background, I'd thought. 'Not another Slaney carry-on.'
ZITA	(*coming back with the drinks*) If the quack knew how much you knock back ...
SLANEY	If he knew how much I need it. Small talk turning me into a screaming mess. UPVC windows versus hardwood. That can last hours, that can. And then we get onto venetian blinds. (*He shudders.*)

ZITA   Come on, then. What's the surprise? It's bath
            night tonight, remember.

SLANEY   My old Mum used to say, 'Only dirty people
            bath.'

ZITA   What did she do, dry clean?

SLANEY   A strip wash she called it. When everyone
            else was in bed.

ZITA   My God, you were poor.

SLANEY   That's right, you laugh.

ZITA   (*exasperated*) What's the surprise, Slaney?

            (*His courage fails.*)

SLANEY   Nothing.

ZITA   What?

SLANEY   Nothing. (*Airily.*) I was lying.

ZITA   One day, one bloody day, Slaney, I will
            strangle you. (ZITA *goes off briefly but
            immediately returns, and slams a wheelchair up to
            the chair, banging down the foot rests.*)

SLANEY   Christ! Face blacking and a balaclava and
            we'd be right back with the SAS scaling that
            embassy.

ZITA   Thanks. Believe me that's what it feels like,
            too. That really is what my bloody life feels
            like!

SLANEY   Right! Right! That's it! I don't want a bath! I
            will not have a bath! I will not be ministered
            to by a fucking martyr.

ZITA   (*angry*) Slaney! I can't cope with this tonight!

SLANEY   (*roars*) No! (*Then, childlike.*) You (*the chair*)
            banged into me.

ZITA   (*flopping down, exhausted*) Oh, God.

            (*They are silent for a moment.*)

SLANEY	Get us a top up, there's a good girl. (*Wearily she does so, gives it to him.*)
ZITA	I found one of your old ledgers in the store room. 1957.
SLANEY	Still there?
ZITA	I'll bring it home. You can re-live the early days.
SLANEY	I'll come back one day.
ZITA	Of course you will. Once your strength builds up.
SLANEY	I was nearly there. Before that last do.
ZITA	Your office is all ready for you. You'll see when you come for the anniversary. Oh! Before I forget. Ted put that bet on for you. The slip's in my case. 'Bad Boy' and 'Prison Bars'.
SLANEY	Your Mum would have picked the winner.
ZITA	Yes.
SLANEY	That woman had luck.
ZITA	Still has.
SLANEY	I remember a point to point once. Talk about lucky. If that woman had backed the hot dog stand it would've won by a short head.
ZITA	Only a short head?
SLANEY	I backed half a dozen at ten bob a time.
ZITA	I remember.
SLANEY	And won nothing.
ZITA	And she backed a hopeless hack and made ten quid. Yes.
SLANEY	Before you were born.

ZITA   I was there. Chucked it down all day and you kept on and on moaning about the car parking fee.

SLANEY   A quid! A quid a car and it was only a muddy bloody field in the middle of Salisbury plain. A lot of money then, a quid. I don't remember you being there.

ZITA   I've got photos of me and Mum by the winners enclosure. Proof.

SLANEY   Alright . . .

ZITA   It was my birthday treat, actually. Nine years old and horse mad. So I was there.

SLANEY   God. Alright, alright, don't go on.

(She takes his glass and refills both of them. She turns around, smiling brightly, hands SLANEY *his drink and sits down.)*

SLANEY   *(encouraged by her smile)* I sacked the Slaney sitter.

*(*ZITA *hears, falters and then ignores what he's said.)*

ZITA   *(still smiling)* Tell you who came in today, that old salesman, the one with the glass eye.

SLANEY   I said, I sacked Mrs Wilson.

ZITA   He said to give you his best and he might pop in one day if he's passing.

SLANEY   Please. It's not a joke. Not a game. I'm serious. I sacked Mrs Wilson.

*(*ZITA *gazes at him in disbelief.)*

SLANEY   It's true. She's leaving at the end of the week.

ZITA   *(snatching at hope)* She hasn't gone yet, then?

SLANEY   No, but she will. I knew if I discussed it with you —

ZITA	Did you upset her? What did you say? Did you swear at her?
SLANEY	No! It was me sacked her not the other way round. I put an advert in the job centre. By phone.
ZITA	Wait a minute ...
SLANEY	She really didn't mind, Zita. Helped me to word it, in fact.
ZITA	You sacked Mrs Wilson and advertised for someone else?
SLANEY	I've advertised for a man. That's what I realised! Don't you see? A man!
ZITA	A man! Slaney, you've had men. The social services sent a man, just one hour a week, but still, a man. You couldn't stand him. The volunteers sent a man and you said he was a half-wit. The Duke of Edinburgh Award scheme sent a whole bloody troop of eager young men and you damn near reduced them to tears. What's changed all of a sudden?
SLANEY	Someone who can push me out for walks. The social services bloke wouldn't do that.
ZITA	His job description didn't include –
SLANEY	(over her) Clean the windows. Everything. It could make your life so much easier, couldn't it?
ZITA	Oh, yes, one long picnic.
SLANEY	(frantic) Someone who can push me up Lovell Hill. Lift me. Someone who does the horses perhaps. Who can get me up the stairs for Christ's sake, so I can look out of a different bloody window once in a while. You'll hurt yourself. One day you'll hurt yourself lifting me. How long is it since you went out

with a man friend? I'm always sitting here
like a bloody gargoyle when you get back –
no wonder you don't see them twice.

ZITA   Thanks, Slaney, I had noticed.

SLANEY   A man could have me all ready for bed by
the time you came home.

ZITA   Oh, I will still come home then, will I? I
won't be totally redundant once you've got
this all powerful all wonderful bloody man?

SLANEY   I knew you'd be like this – that's why we
ended up with a bloody dry run yesterday
and ... (*He runs out of steam.*) I thought that
you'd be glad to have a bit of help, Zita,
that's all.

ZITA   You let me clean the house, cook the food,
take over the business, but by God, you won't
let me get near you.

SLANEY   It's not like that. Is it so terrible to want a
man around me?

ZITA   (*trying to find normality*) What sort of man?

SLANEY   Just an ordinary bloke. Why not?

ZITA   Because you're kidding yourself, Dad.
Because it's not going to be like that ...

SLANEY   No?

ZITA   – because *I'm* the only one who accepts the
tantrums and the carry on of life with the
witty devil-may-care Slaney! Not volunteers.
Not your wife and my Mother. Just me.

(*Pause.*)

ZITA   (*quieter*) There are limits to what people will
do for money.

SLANEY   Thanks. I want another drink.

ZITA	You've had enough.
SLANEY	I want another drink. Christ, I want another drink. Watch my lips, I want another drink. I want –
ZITA	Alright, alright. (*She sloshes out two more whiskies.*) I suppose that you want a chess player, because I never did learn, did I?
SLANEY	I don't care about chess.
ZITA	A masochistic sports loving horse betting chess player.
SLANEY	The world used to be full of them.
ZITA	Oh, please –
SLANEY	Advertise for one now and see where it gets you! I want someone I can sink my teeth into and not feel guilty about it afterwards. I want a football hooligan. A punk. A moron with psychotic tendencies. Someone I can yell at.
ZITA	Wonderful. I'll be able to go to work with never a worry in the world.
SLANEY	So that when you come home I've got something to tell you about. Not all one way! An evening of what they said to you and you said to them. Never having anything to tell you in return. Zita, you're sick of the games and carry-on – can you imagine how sick of it all I am? (*Pause.*) Hearing about all the bloody nonsense. Champagne and smoked salmon! Celebrating the day Slaney Printers became Slaney Printers plc. The day this happened to me.
ZITA	Oh, God. It wasn't the day –
SLANEY	OK. Two years later. But the same day. To me. The one caused the other.
ZITA	If you hadn't been at loggerheads with the other directors all the time.

SLANEY   Bloody plc. And you're celebrating it.

ZITA   Is that what this is all about? Is it? So, all
              peeved and hard done by, you've gone and
              sacked Mrs Wilson. That makes perfect sense.

SLANEY   (*shouting*) I had to do something. Hurt
              someone. I had to prove that I can still
              decide things for myself. (*Pleading.*) And it's
              not just that. I want to make things better for
              you.

ZITA   Oh, Slaney, I've not complained. When Mum
              walked out on you, when you had the first
              stroke, when you moved in here, I've never
              complained, have I?

SLANEY   No, but –

ZITA   You're the one with the daily never ending
              list of moans and groans.

SLANEY   I haven't got any moans. If anything my life
              is too good. Too cosseted. Too smooth and
              untroubled. That's what I'm trying to tell
              you.

ZITA   I look forward to coming home, to the games
              and the tricks and the tantrums.

SLANEY   (*placatory*) And I look forward to your coming
              home. Christ, if we're both so bloody happy,
              how is it we're so fucking miserable?

              (*The lights fade.*)

Scene Three

It's evening. SLANEY *sits waiting, expectant, with restrained
excitement.* ZITA *rustles around him, sharp and unhappy.*

SLANEY   The place is fine. I said, the place is fine.

ZITA   I wish they'd told you his age. I mean, what's
              the point if he's seventeen?

SLANEY	He won't be seventeen. 'Mature' I said to them, the job centre. (*Sees her moving something for the second time.*) For Christ's sake!
ZITA	He could be seventeen years old with an earring for all you know. That'd get the blood pressure soaring, wouldn't it?
SLANEY	I am not an uncontrollable idiot, Zita.
ZITA	And don't make your decision straight away. Tell him you'll let him know –
SLANEY	I have interviewed people before – Here's someone now.
ZITA	I can't hear – (*The doorbell sounds.*)
SLANEY	That's him!
ZITA	Ask him for two references.
SLANEY	I know.
ZITA	And don't make your decision –
SLANEY	Zita!

(*She goes to the door and opens it.* REG *stands there, in his interview best.*)

ZITA	Mr Dalton ... Please come in. I'm Zita, we spoke on the phone.
REG	Ah! Yes! Thank you. Saw these houses going up. Coupla years back. First time I've been in one, though. Used to walk round the estate before the doors were on, through the breeze block walls, imagine what the places'd be like.
ZITA	Well – here it is.
REG	It was the board they put up 'Executive Residences'. Wanted to see what they were. (*He sees* SLANEY *at last and walks forward with a big smile.*)
ZITA	Mr Dalton, this is my father, Jack Slaney.
REG	How d'you do, Mr Slaney?

SLANEY	Wonderful.
ZITA	Well. Tea or coffee, Mr Dalton?
REG	Reg. Please call me Reg. No. Thank you.
ZITA	Oh. Right. I'll just pop upstairs, then. I've got a few bits and bobs to be getting on with. (*She exits.*)
SLANEY	Well, then, sit down and tell me about yourself.
REG	Well ... Straight in with the trick question. (*Sees that* SLANEY *isn't smiling.*) Thirty six. Divorced. Been a warehouseman most of my life.
SLANEY	Why'd you stop?
REG	Fletcher's packed in. Closed down.
SLANEY	Go on.
REG	Been what you could call unemployed on and off for a few years. Trouble is, warehouses now, cut backs, see, and computers. Fletcher's, we used to hand pick off order forms. Had a few jobs since, 'course, but nothing long term. Tried bricklaying, enjoyed that, well, labouring for a brickie it was. Still, I did enjoy that. Erm. Three kids. Only the wife's got them. Ex-wife. I moved out, see. Seemed the best thing to do. Give the wife and the kids the house. Ex-wife.
SLANEY	Where do you live now?
REG	Got a room. By the station. I don't know. Been working twenty years and I end up with all my worldly goods in two suitcases and a carrier bag. Funny old world, innit?
SLANEY	I laugh all the time.
REG	Imagined youngsters in these places somehow. Bloke with a briefcase and a Sierra, wife with a hair-do, you know. Still.

SLANEY	Why do you want this job?
REG	I can't just stay at home all the time. And with it being one room just, well, anything's better. Companion and assistant, it said, and I thought, 'Give it a go'. That's all, really.
SLANEY	(*looking away, bored*) Ah.
REG	So, here I am. Large as life. (*He breaks off, recognising that* SLANEY *is being rude and then speaks with a bite.*) Do you want me to go?
SLANEY	What I am looking for is some hint about your character. How we'll get on together, hour after hour. What we'll find to talk about. What we could do with ourselves.
REG	Well ... (*Looking around.*) Dunno, off hand. What do you do now? (SLANEY *shrugs.*) Bit pokey, innit?
SLANEY	Built for a young couple, with a Sierra and a hair-do.
REG	How do you get to the loo?
SLANEY	We had an extension built. Bedsitting room, bath, shower, chair lift, the lot. The only thing we haven't got is a Sinclair C5.
REG	Bet you get sick of it. Don't you ever feel like just cutting loose, getting out of here and having a good – what – explosion, like? A swear up?
SLANEY	A swear up?
REG	What I do. When I'm sick of the four walls and the sight of that bloody Baby Belling with its one saucepan – go for a walk and have a good swear up. Up on the hills. Shout anything I want to into the wind. You can't do that, I suppose. Tell you what, I could take you up there. The two of us. Having a swear up together, eh? If you fancy it. Got a dog?

SLANEY   What? No.

REG   You get one if you want one. I'll exercise it.
            Do you both at the same time, see. I mean, if
            you take me on. So. There's just you and
            your daughter, then, is there?

SLANEY   I'm divorced.

REG   So am I. Who needs it, eh?

SLANEY   I do. I miss my wife. I miss my job. I dislike
            hearing about how well the works is doing
            without me. Better than it ever did with me.
            I miss the men. I miss the abuse and the
            laughter of the print shop. I loathe the new
            world and all the clever bloody people it's
            spawned. I hate it so much that when my
            company went public I took one look at the
            board of directors and had a stroke. I am not
            a happy soul. I do not require being made
            into one. And I don't want to be 'done' at the
            same time as a dog. I just think that we
            should get a few things straight.

REG   Oh. Right.

SLANEY   You saw my daughter. When I was first ill,
            three years ago, she was twenty-one. Now,
            she tells me, she is forty. How do you feel
            about being sixty?

REG   Well ...

SLANEY   The job would be extremely tedious. I am
            short tempered, I throw things and I have
            amazing methane ladened wind. (*He ends on a
            note of triumph and challenge.*)

REG   Well ... We're none of us perfect. (SLANEY
            stares at him in disbelief.) That's what I say.

SLANEY   Oh, God.

REG   We all get a black-on at times.

SLANEY   (*in growing desperation*) Are you a political
            animal?

REG   Political?

SLANEY   Who do you support?

REG   I don't vote, mate. All as bad as each other,
            that's what I say.

SLANEY   Is it? If Scargill was back in favour and led
            another strike, and he was on TV every five
            minutes, wearing that bloody silly baseball
            cap, would you say anything?

REG   Say anything?

SLANEY   If he came on and said, "Let me just say this,
            Mr Walden, I will say just one thing ... "
            would you react at all? Have anything to say?

REG   Walden doesn't do the news, does he? I think
            I'd say, "Oh, look, I didn't know he did the
            news."

SLANEY   (*heavily*) You answer the door to this chinless
            young solicitor – unmarried, lives two
            hundred miles away, you can see his white
            Golf GTi out in the road – he's the
            Conservative candidate, asking for your vote.
            What would you say?

            (*Pause.*)

REG   I'm sorry, I only work here ... and I'd ask if
            you wanted to speak to him.

SLANEY   Do you have any bloody opinions at all? Do
            you support a football club?

REG   No.

SLANEY   Are you a member of CND?

REG   No!

SLANEY   The PLO, then? Listen. A bloody great bomb
            goes off in the next street killing twenty-five
            children and old ladies. The IRA claims

responsibility from fucking Dublin, large as life, and says it was all a mistake. You come in that morning and I'm foaming at the mouth and throwing things at the telly on which is the face of a Sinn Fein spokesman.

What do you say to me?

REG   What, you're really upset, are you?

SLANEY   Of course I'm bloody upset. They've just killed twenty-five sodding people. They've said "Oops. Sorry!" The blast cracked my fucking window. Of course I'm upset. (*He yells.*) Zita! Zita! I'm sorry, Mr . . .

REG   Dalton. Reg Dalton.

SLANEY   Yes. I'm sorry. (*Yelling.*) Zita! (ZITA *comes down the stairs.*)

ZITA   That didn't take long.

SLANEY   Mr Dalton is a Mary Poppins fan.

ZITA   I'm sorry?

SLANEY   He very kindly offered to teach me to shout obscenities into the wind.

REG   Not obscenities –

SLANEY   Up on the hills. I don't know how well we would get on, actually. And he wants us to get an Irish Wolfhound.

ZITA   Don't be silly. I am sorry, Mr Dalton –

SLANEY   So that he could do me and the dog at the same time!

ZITA   Slaney, you're being very rude to Mr Dalton.

SLANEY   Call him Reg.

REG   Hang on a minute—

SLANEY	And he does accept that no one's perfect.
REG	I came here, in all honesty – ready to be perfectly nice –
SLANEY	Mistake number one!
REG	Your daughter had said on the phone how difficult you could be.
SLANEY	"Childish". I know.
REG	And I thought, poor old sod. Make allowances.
SLANEY	I thought you might have thought that.
REG	I been for some bloody awful jobs. Jobs people like you and her don't ever have to think about. Tanners piling up sheep skins in stinking filthy huts. Incinerator man at the hospital. All sorts. Washing pig gut for traditional sausages. 'Real' sausage, the sort you get in a 'real' shop with dark green paintwork and the name picked out in gold. The butcher wears a striped pinny. I could've done any of them jobs. A trained rottweiller could've done most of 'em. I'd do any ruddy thing, I would. Tell me what to do and I'll do it. Jump through a hoop? Here I go.
ZITA	I'm sure my father didn't mean to –
REG	But this has to be the worst sodding job so far. You sitting there like Buddha while she skips around you. Like the ruddy King and I.
SLANEY	Without the music.
REG	Ready to do any damn thing you wanted, I was. But just not up to your little games. What did you want me to say?
SLANEY	I didn't want you to say anything. To be something. A personality, that's what I want.
REG	An applicant. That's what I am.

SLANEY	Not what I want!
REG	I can be anyone. Anything. Workfare. Turn into anything at the click of a finger, or the launch of another scheme. Anything.
SLANEY	(*mimic*) Nobody's perfect! ... We all have our off days ...
REG	Saying what I thought you wanted me to. Say anything me, do anything. One factory closes down and another opens. Tell 'em what they want to hear to get the job, any job. Labourer today, driver tomorrow, security guard next week. Available for any job, anywhere. Maggie's ideal man, me. You have no idea what sort of a nasty sod I am, have you? You have no idea what sort of a bastard I really am.
ZITA	Please ...
SLANEY	And you have no idea what sort of a bastard I really am.
REG	Oh, but I do. You're a crippled bastard.

(*There's a shocked silence and slowly* SLANEY *grins.*)

ZITA	Right. That's enough.
SLANEY	He'll do.
ZITA	Slaney!
SLANEY	Starting Monday!
ZITA	The references, Slaney!
SLANEY	(*roaring*) I'm doing the fucking interview! Starting Monday! (*Suddenly anxious and vulnerable.*) Monday?
REG	Monday.

ZITA   Oh, God! You haven't got references, you
                haven't even got his address, have you?
                Still . . . well done Slaney! Anything,
                apparently, is better than me! (*She runs off.*)

Scene Four

Late evening. SLANEY *and* ZITA *are watching TV. The light from
the television flickers on their faces. Empty whisky glasses and a
half empty bottle between them.* SLANEY *is ready for bed but
wearing an old fashioned smoking jacket.* ZITA *turns off the TV.*

ZITA   You look very distinguished in that.

SLANEY   Don't I? He said it would make me look less
                like an invalid. Be a bit more cheerful for
                you.

ZITA   Well, it's a hundred times better than striped
                pyjamas.

SLANEY   I like striped pyjamas. What are you doing?

ZITA   I told you. Checking the guest list. Four
                weeks to go.

SLANEY   Bloody nonsense. Chucking good money
                away.

ZITA   That's it. Finis. Apparently the caterers do it
                all very nicely. Silver service and all that. If
                you want it, of course. Black frocks and white
                aprons for the waitresses and little monkey
                jackets for the men.

SLANEY   Bloody hell. Now it's caterers.

ZITA   I told you. Phillipinos from the big cleaning
                agencies. And domestic work I suppose,
                Moonlighting.

SLANEY   Poor sods.

ZITA   They'll get paid. The woman who brought
                the menus, one of the partners, said that
                they'll do all the hours they can get. Dirt
                cheap, too.

SLANEY   And you're happy about that?

ZITA   Slaney, they tendered for the job and they
            were the best buy. How they do
            it ... Anyway, it was a board decision. Let's
            not row. We haven't had an arguement for
            days and days.

            (*There is a moment's silence as she packs her things
            away.*)

ZITA   That was such a peaceful evening. I do feel
            spoiled, coming home to you all bathed and
            pink and shiny, a casserole in the oven, the
            place tidy. Do you know, I've read two books
            in the ten days he's been here.

SLANEY   Wonderful.

ZITA   You seem much quieter too. Do you feel
            quieter?

SLANEY   Bloody exhausted.

ZITA   Really? Well, isn't that good?

SLANEY   Is it?

ZITA   You always complained that you couldn't
            sleep at night. Couldn't feel sleepy even. I
            think you were quite right, you know. What
            you needed *was* Reg. I mean, look at us now.
            We've had a super relaxing evening and a
            civilised meal, we'll both get a good night's
            sleep, and in the morning I'll stay in bed
            until half seven and then I'll bring you coffee
            in bed and he'll get you up later and –

SLANEY   Zita, why are you telling me all this?

ZITA   Well. It is good, isn't it? It is working out,
            having Reg here, isn't it? And he's very
            willing, isn't he? Slaney?
            (REG *enters, dresses* SLANEY *up for the outside,
            not taking off the pyjamas, just covering his legs
            with a rug once he's in his wheelchair. He wheels
            him off briskly ready for the next scene.*)

As the next scene sets up:

ZITA *goes to stand in front of a mirror, slips out of her dress and into another one. She brushes her hair, slowly, counting the strokes. She begins to make up carefully. Peers at her reflection, squinty eyed, as if trying to see herself in soft focus. She smiles at herself gently, as if to a lover.*

Scene Five

REG *is pushing* SLANEY *up the hill above the town. It's cold and windy.*

SLANEY *is wrapped up well against the weather but* REG *is wearing old jeans, a T-shirt and a cheap bomber jacket. It's hard work pushing* SLANEY *up such a steep slope.*

REG   G'arn, ya bugger. G'arn.

              (*He bellows into the wind.*)

              G'arn Pull, Slaney, pull. Lean forward!

              (*They pause at the top of the hill and* REG *hangs over the back of the chair breathlessly.*)

              Oh, my Christ. Oh, Gawd. That's better. Look at that then. Look at that! Innit marvellous? Slaney. Look.

SLANEY   I can see nothing with you going on and on and bloody on.

              (*Pause.*)

REG   Listen. The silence. Like someone's shut the door on the world. Like the telly, one minute you hear street noise and music and God knows what then someone shuts the cardboard door in the scenery and it all stops like magic.

SLANEY   I'm cold.

REG   Kills the germs. And then, slowly, you realise that there is a noise. The silent noise of a wind that never stops.

SLANEY	(*appalled at the line*) My God.
REG	Whenever you come up here, whatever the weather, the wind is always there. Alright. Go on. Tell me. What's wrong?
SLANEY	I don't think that this is working out.
REG	Only thing is, according to Zita it's working out 'ever so well'. Innit? Feels years younger she told me. Like a weight had come off of her shoulders. Looks forward to coming home now, she says.
SLANEY	She always did.
REG	Yeah? Still, what does she know? And she'll get over it. Soon be back in the swing of it all. I mean, she done it for three years, why not for another thirty?
SLANEY	This isn't a chronic condition.
REG	No. Course not. You're just not going to get any better.
SLANEY	Physio—
REG	According to the physiotherapist, that is. Disappointing, that's the word she used. After you made such headway with the other strokes. Still. Zita can manage.
SLANEY	I'll get someone else. You'll get something else.
REG	Oh, yes, I'll get something else. Vacancies all over the shop. More vacancies than ever before, they tell me. (*Suddenly hard.*) I thought you wanted a bastard? Someone you could get your teeth into? Didn't you say that?
SLANEY	It isn't working out like that. I want to go home.

REG   Already? We've only just got here. Nothing
             to rush back for, is there? No one standing at
             the door with a rolling pin, is there? No one
             to give a bugger. Funny to think, me
             divorced and you divorced. One in three
             marriages now.

SLANEY   Five.

REG   Five in three? Getting worse then, eh? Once
             you and me could've been allies, you know.
             Yeah. I was all for everyone, me. The
             proverbial chirpy workman, salt of the earth.
             I could do everything, fork lift, stock take,
             despatch, everything. And even after
             Fletcher's shut, on that site, labouring for the
             brickie, it was alright. He did a lot of fancy
             stuff, you know. "Arches and curved
             retaining walls a speciality." I loved watching
             him. People don't realise the team work,
             brickie and mate, running up ladders with
             hods piled high. Makes a difference to a
             brickie, a good mate does. We got on OK. I
             was as brown as ... Still ... And you, bet
             you was a good sort of bloke to work for,
             weren't you? Prided yourself on it.

SLANEY   I did my best.

REG   Got on OK with the workers, eh?

SLANEY   I knew their families. Knew which kids were
             struggling at school, which wives were
             pregnant. Worked for me whole life-times,
             they did. I knew them and they knew me.
             Knew.

REG   Yeah. Those were the ... Sometimes I can't
             remember the order of things, you know.
             What I was doing when. Where I lived when.
             How old the kids are. Got used to not
             remembering their faces now. They've sort of
             merged, the three of them, into one small,
             blond kid, crying. Always crying when I try

to remember. You'd think you'd remember
your own children. Still. There you are. I had
this job lined up once in an industrial estate.
Big exhaust fitters. Went in for the first day,
like they'd said, and the place was deserted.
The big notices was all there still. 'Can't get
quicker than a nit wit flicker.' Gives it a
whole new meaning. The whole road was
deserted. The whole estate. See, it was an
enterprise zone. Or an inner-city zone or
something. You know, articles in the paper,
speech by the MP and all that. Then,
whatever it was had run out of time. All the
do-it-yourself superstores and carpet
warehouses had moved over to the other side
of town, another enterprise zone, I suppose.
Champagne opening all over again. Only
they'd forgotten to tell me.

SLANEY   I'm sorry. Sorry things are like they are.

REG   One more day, one more chance, a finger in
             every pie. Owning everything, responsible for
             nothing. That's what it's all about now,
             people who think like that.

SLANEY   Worse thing I ever did. 'Public liability
             company'! Talked into it. Glossy bloody
             hand-outs. Worse thing I ever did, worse
             days work ... And even if I do ever go back,
             what will I do? It's not my print shop
             anymore. All computers and machines
             and ...   I'm sorry things are like they are.

REG   I'll be alright. I'll get summat else. Perhaps a
             shop job. They come and go dead easy.
             Wearing plastic badges 'My name is Reg', and
             selling boxes. That's what they do now, these
             shops. Don't need much training for that.
             You go in and you ask for a computer or a
             telly or something, and they fetch the box.
             They don't know anything about what's

inside it. Selling ruddy boxes with writing on
the sides. "Can I have a P3000 telly, please?"
"What colour box is it in? Blue? Oh yeah,
here's one of them. Hang on, I'll give it a
shake and make sure it isn't empty."
Customer service that is.

SLANEY   You're still a young man. You could still
           build something – a career.

REG   (*laughs, a denial*) The two of us, sitting up
           here in the wind, trees without roots. Have to
           mind we don't blow away, eh? Fallen oaks.
           Thinks a lot of you, old Zita does. Her clever
           old man. Opening his own print shop,
           watching it grow till it's the biggest and best
           in the whole bloody Midlands.

SLANEY   It was better when it was half the size.

REG   Daddy's girl. Slaney's girl. You and her
           together in that nice little house. For years.
           Old women sitting by you all day long, and in
           the evenings – Zita.

SLANEY   I'll get someone else –

REG   Sneaked me in the back way, didn't you? If I
           go I reckon it's back to the women, clickety
           click.

SLANEY   Shut up!

REG   Do you want that?

           (*Pause.*)

SLANEY   No.

REG   Stuck with me then, eh? Shout!

SLANEY   What?

REG   Shout into the wind! Come on. Together.
           Shout! Shout! Shout!

SLANEY   (*loudly over him*) I don't want to shout.

REG   (*shouting to the sky*) Bastards! You can't touch
               me! You can't do it! You can't touch me 'cos
               I won't *be* touched. Here I am! Come and get
               me!

               (*He stops and looks at* SLANEY.) Shout, then.

               (*He takes the blanket off* SLANEY's *legs and turns
               away.*) Come on! Try and get me! Don't give
               a (*He raises two fingers.*) Don't give a (*One
               finger.*) Don't give a bloody monkey's arse!
               (*He crows with joy.*)

SLANEY   (*calm*) What do you do in the summer?

REG   Whatever's going on down there right now,
               in all them office blocks, whatever they're
               dreaming up, it can't touch us. What do you
               mean, "What do I do in the summer"?

SLANEY   When the sun's shining and all the little
               kiddies are up here with their Mummys and
               all the old ladies are walking their dogs. What
               do you do about shouting then?

REG   I do without, mate.

SLANEY   I'm cold.

REG   Then bloody shout! (*He takes* SLANEY's *scarf,
               puts it on.*) Shout!

SLANEY   I bloody won't.

               (REG *takes his hat.*)

REG   You bloody will. Let it all out. Give it merry,
               sodding hell. The rage of the helpless, the
               hopeless, the terminally bloody ineffectual.
               You will. Eventually. Shout!

               (*Pause.*)

               Fair enough. Please yourself. The kiosk's
               open.

               (*He walks away.*)

SLANEY	Where are you going?
REG	Styrofoam tea.
SLANEY	You can't leave me up here. I'm freezing!
REG	Can't hear you!
SLANEY	(*shouting*) Leave me here, then. I like it here. Better than listening to your bleating. Bleat bleat bleat.
REG	(*off*) Louder! Louder!
SLANEY	You can't hurt me! Bugger off, then!
REG	G'arn Slaney. Dance my dance and sing my tune!
SLANEY	Bastard!
REG	One more time. Have a bloody good shout up!
SLANEY	(*quieter*) Oh, Christ. I'm cold. Reg. I'm so cold.

(*The lights gradually dim as* REG *comes back on, he chucks* SLANEY'S *clothes into his lap and wheels him off.*)

Scene Six

As the lights go down on the hill so they rise in the house, where ZITA *hears a noise off, and gets herself ready. As the door opens and* REG *wheels* SLANEY *in, she runs over just as if she hadn't been waiting.*

ZITA	Hello you two!
SLANEY	(*delighted*) Zita! What are you doing home?
ZITA	Well, I had to go and see about the flowers for the 'do' and it was only four so I thought, blow it, I'll have an early finish for once. Hello, Reg.
REG	Hello, Zita. You weren't wearing that this morning, were you?

ZITA	No. Fancy you noticing.
SLANEY	You could be off home, then, Reg.
REG	I'm not in a rush. I'll sort you out before I go.
SLANEY	I don't want you to. I want Zita.
ZITA	Slaney! I know! While you do Slaney I'll get a meal ready and we can all eat together for a change. (*Then, to* SLANEY.) While Reg is giving you your bath I'll make us a lovely salad and some nice home made pizza.
SLANEY	Lovely lovely. Nice nice. You never used to talk like that. (*Seeing her for the first time.*) Why are you all dolled up?
ZITA	I'm not. Honestly!
SLANEY	I don't want him to stay. Our evenings are our evenings.
REG	(*quietly*) We had a bit of a tantrum I'm afraid.
ZITA	What's the matter with you?
SLANEY	Cold. I got cold up on that bloody hill.
ZITA	It's not that cold. And you're ever so well wrapped up.
REG	A nice warm bath. He'll feel better after a nice warm bath.
	(*He wheels* SLANEY *off into the bathroom.*)
ZITA	That's the idea! You always feel better after a nice warm bath.
	(*She begins to prepare the meal. The sound of water running is heard off.* REG *returns, rolling up his sleeves.*)
REG	He's on the loo. I appreciate this, you know.
ZITA	It's nothing. I just suddenly thought how nice it would be.

REG	Be lovely. I don't cook for myself.
ZITA	You mustn't let him upset you. He's used to snapping at people. Well, at me really. I never minded, you see. Understood, I suppose ...
REG	I understand, too. Don't worry.
ZITA	(*in a rush*) Your interview. I wouldn't want you to think –
REG	What?
ZITA	I wasn't against you. It must have seemed that I was against you coming here but –
REG	Don't worry about it.
SLANEY	(*off*) Reg! Are you bloody coming?
REG	(*going*) Alright, alright, just passing the time of day with Zita, that's all.

(*On the way off, he pauses and winks at her.*)

Us below stairs must be allowed our little privileges. (*He exits.*)

(*Smiling and dreamy,* ZITA *continues with the meal. There are sounds from the bathroom. She pauses and wanders to the doorway, listening.*)

REG	(*off*) Hup-la! Up you get! And in you ... go! (*Splash.*) There now, isn't that lovely?
SLANEY	I like my baths deep.
REG	Waste of money that.
SLANEY	I always have deep hot baths. (*Growing childish.*) I keep telling you that.
REG	Nice and warm but never hot and four inches of water is quite enough.
SLANEY	I like to soak. It helps me to relax.
REG	Relax? You spend your whole flamin' life relaxing, you do.

SLANEY	My neck aches, my shoulders –
REG	'My arse and my elbow'. Yes, I know, a miracle of modern science you are. 'We have the technology, we can re-build this man!'

(REG *hums a 60's pop song. Water splashes.* ZITA *makes as if to go into them and checks herself.*)

REG	Come on, now, stop pouting. Be a good Slaney, sit forward while I do your back.

(ZITA *slowly walks away.*)

SLANEY	That's too cold! It's too bloody cold!

(ZITA *turns on the radio and busies herself.*)

Zita!

(*She turns her back.*)

REG	There now. You do the naughty bits.

(REG *stands in the doorway to the bathroom, sleeves rolled up, looking towards the kitchen but talking to* SLANEY.)

Nice house, this. Homely. Not that I'd know. Funny though, the way I can't remember my kids. For the life of me. They've merged, the three of them, into one small, blond kid, crying. Always crying when I try to remember.

SLANEY	I've finished.
REG	I suppose the youngest is school age. Teenage Mutant Ninja Turtles T-shirt and little blue shorts forever falling down.
SLANEY	Am I to sit here all bloody night?
REG	Gap toothed, hopping home, running ahead. You know, like they do. But I can't see his face.
SLANEY	(*louder*) I'm cold!

(*Sighing,* REG *goes in to* SLANEY.)

REG   Used to play with them in the bath. Ducks
            and things. Submarines.

SLANEY   (*yelling*) I'm cold!

            (*Lights fade.*)

ACT TWO

A week later.

SLANEY'S *bed is visible at the back of the set, in another room, an ordinary divan but with a 'davit' over it and a handle to pull himself up with.*

Scene Seven

SLANEY, ZITA *and* REG *are sitting around after the meal.* REG *is making a gesture towards moving, but not actually going.*

REG   Well. Nice as this is, it won't buy the baby any bonnets.

SLANEY A new bonnet.

REG   Sorry?

SLANEY The phrase is, 'This won't buy the baby a new bonnet.'

     (ZITA *and* REG *exchange glances of sympathy.*)

ZITA   (*rising*) Have another coffee, Reg.

REG   It's getting late ... but go on, then.

     (ZITA *goes to the kitchen.* SLANEY *silently mimes the words and* REG *sees.*)

REG   You're very quiet tonight, Slaney.

SLANEY Watching the cabaret. The steps in the dance.

REG   (*to* SLANEY) Might learn something, then.

ZITA   (*off, calling through*) Learn something?

REG   I was just saying, I got a book out of the library, about strokes.

ZITA   (*returning*) That was good of you.

REG   Intellectual impairment is rare, but the emotions do get tangled. Sort of made raw. Near the surface, it said.

(ZITA *is uncomfortable speaking about* SLANEY *in front of him, but tries to make it normal and bright.*)

ZITA   I think that we've found that out, haven't we? Well, I think so, anyway.

REG   It said that the biggest impact was likely to be upon the family.

SLANEY   Surely not the biggest?

REG   The victim can become inward looking and self-absorbed, not recognising the increased burden and load on others.

ZITA   Oh, I don't think –

REG   (*remembering*) Childlike, it said. Recommended facing the problem squarely and talking about it honestly. 'You're an adult so we'll discuss things with you, adult to adult.' Only right, when you think of it.

ZITA   (*uncertainly*) Yes.

SLANEY   Who wrote it?

REG   What?

SLANEY   Who wrote the fucking book?

ZITA   Slaney!

REG   I believe it's an American woman.

SLANEY   Oh, well, there you are then. That lot could wring a new philosophy from a snot rag and a science from a fart.

ZITA   Slaney! Honestly!

SLANEY   I'm tired.

REG   And that's another thing. She said it was a bad thing for an invalid to take over the living space of the family.

SLANEY   What family?

REG   Becoming, it said, the centre of the
             household, so that all life within the home
             went on around his disability, and was
             affected by it.

SLANEY   Bollocks.

ZITA   Goodness, you took it all in, anyway.

REG   Get quick at picking things up, see.

SLANEY   Just think, all those years wasted at
             university. Hand out a few paperbacks and
             we could set a match to Oxford, turn
             Cambridge into a theme park.

REG   So I was thinking ...

SLANEY   Here it comes–

REG   How would it be if I was to put him to bed
             every evening before you came home?

ZITA   At four o' clock?

REG   I could stay on till six. He's got a telly in
             there. That's all he does of an evening, isn't
             it, Slaney?

SLANEY   We talk.

REG   You could go and sit with him if you wanted
             to, couldn't you?

ZITA   Yes ... but ...

REG   Think about it. Anyway, I'm here tonight, so
             I can do the honours this once, can't I?
             (*Bringing up the wheelchair and helping him into
             it.*) And lifting him in and out of this
             wheelchair can't be doing you any good.
             Think about it.

SLANEY   You could put in a baby alarm and a tape of
             womb noises for when I get emotionally raw.

REG   (*going*) Come on now, Slaney, be fair. Don't
             take it out on Zee.

SLANEY   (*off*) Zita. Her name's Zita.

REG   Look at this, the bed all turned back and
         ready for you, the electric blanket on.
         (*Helping him onto his bed.*) There you are – all
         snug and warm. Want the telly on?

Scene Eight

When the lights come up it is a week later. SLANEY *is in bed and* ZITA
is preparing the evening meal of soup.

REG   (*entering from* SLANEY's *room*) Good as gold
         and as snug as a bug. Bit more civilised in
         here now, isn't it? None of his papers and
         chess pieces and all that rammel.

ZITA   It's transformed. Well, not the room, the
         evenings.

REG   (*seeing two places set*) You don't have to get me
         tea every night, you know.

ZITA   I like to. I don't want to eat on my own
         anyway.

REG   You shouldn't be waiting on everyone, a
         successful working woman like you.

ZITA   I just run an office.

REG   A company.

ZITA   With help. (*Putting* SLANEY's *tray on the table.*)

REG   And all the extras they want from you. This
         marquee do, champers and little things on
         trays. All that.

ZITA   It's not so bad.

REG   And then home to the ironing, the washing.

ZITA   (*laughing*) Don't go on. I can't help it. The
         way I am. (*Bringing a soup bowl in.*) I'm sorry
         it's only soup and rolls.

REG   Give over. That's grand. Is this his? I'll take
         it.

ZITA   Perhaps I should go.

REG   You rest your legs. You can see him later.

ZITA   Well . . .

REG   Sit down. (*He takes the tray.*)

ZITA   Tell him I'll be in in a little while.

REG   Yes. Yes. Yes.

            (REG *pauses just inside* SLANEY'S *door.* SLANEY
            turns his face away and closes his eyes. REG *sees
            him do this but puts the tray down on the bedside
            cabinet with exaggerated care and tiptoes out.* ZITA
            *spoons the soup into the bowls and pours a whirl of
            cream in each.*)

REG   (*entering briskly*) Look at that. My old woman
            would've poured the stuff out of the
            saucepan and into the dish, and that
            would've been that. Plonk on the table. Half
            a loaf still in its wrapping. Look at that.

ZITA   It's only soup.

REG   A little swirl of cream, a sprinkling of parsley.
            (*Feeling the rolls.*) Hot rolls in starched
            serviettes.

ZITA   It really isn't anything special.

REG   Have we got any pepper?

ZITA   Oh. Sorry. (*She goes off and returns with the
            pepper mill.*)

REG   Thanks love. Now, sit down and have yours,
            you're not my servant, you know. Fact,
            looking at it square, I'm your servant in a
            sort of way.

ZITA   Don't be silly. You don't know what a
            pleasure it is to have someone who
            appreciates things. All Slaney wants is pie
            and chips and arguments.

REG   He's looking better, isn't he?

ZITA   He's lost that weight the doctor was nagging
        us about. And his skin looks so much clearer.
        All that fresh air.

REG   I like to take him up there every day. A
        change of scene. We sit and watch the world
        go by.

ZITA   You are good.

REG   My job.

ZITA   You do so much.

REG   So do you!

ZITA   Not particularly –

REG   Yes you do. Look at you – you've done all
        the career bit but you've managed to stay,
        well, womanly. Feminine. Not many women
        could do that –

ZITA   Oh, I don't ...

REG   I mean, I moan at you for doing the washing
        up and that, but I wouldn't have it any other
        way.

ZITA   No?

REG   I like a woman to be a woman. And you are.
        Am I embarrassing you?

ZITA   (sipping furiously) No. (Rising.) More soup?

REG   Thanks. I have embarrassed you, haven't I?

ZITA   No. (Refilling his bowl.) I'm just not ever so
        good at talking.

REG   Another point in your favour. (She starts.)
        Only joking.

(*He slurps the soup. She watches, fascinated by his masculinity. Finally he throws the spoon into the bowl, clattering.*)

REG   Right. Now. I'll do the washing up.

ZITA   No. Really.

REG   You sit there and put your feet up.

ZITA   I'll go and get Slaney's dishes.

REG   No! (*Laughing now, taking* ZITA *by the elbows and steering her to* SLANEY'S *chair.*) You do what you're told and sit there. I'll get the old sod's dirties. There. Good girl.

(*She sits down, bemused, laughing, girlish.* REG *goes into* SLANEY'S *room.* SLANEY *glares at him and then turns away.* REG *comes out again immediately.*)

REG   Coffee coming up!

ZITA   Did he drink his soup?

REG   Asleep.

ZITA   I'll heat it up for him later.

REG   Up to you.

ZITA   Don't you think I should?

(REG *shrugs.*)

Why not?

REG   Trying to get him into a routine. All the books say that.

ZITA   I'd better go in and see that he's alright.

REG   Look. You said he was so much better, didn't you? Said he was looking good, sleeping better, all that. Didn't you?

ZITA   Of course, you're doing a terrific job.

REG   I'm doing it the best way I know how. If
          you're going to go around after me, checking
          up ... what sort of message is he going to
          get?

ZITA   What?

REG   I'm just saying. Not the sort of job to give a
          bloke any satisfaction ... even me.

ZITA   Reg! I'm sorry. Reg, don't be huffy, please.

REG   Well ... You make me huffy.

ZITA   I know. I'm sorry. My fault. Please. Come
          and sit down.

REG   The coffee.

ZITA   I'll do that. You sit down. (*He does so. They
          cross.*) You've been working too. Would you
          like cheese and biscuits?

REG   Yeah. That'd be nice. A bit of cheese and
          some biscuits.

ZITA   Right! (*Exiting.*) Won't be a minute.

          (ZITA *returns carrying a board of cheese and
          biscuits, puts them on the table. He pats the arm of
          the chair for her to sit down beside him.*)

ZITA   The coffee's perking.

REG   It's not ready yet. Sit down.

          (*She does so, self-consciously.*)

ZITA   I feel like a naughty kid in someone else's
          house. As if he should be here all the time.

REG   You've got lovely hands.

ZITA   When I was in bed last night I realised that I
          hadn't seen him all day. Awake, I mean.
          Worrying about Slaney was never off my
          mind before you came, and now, quite
          suddenly, I realise that I go for whole days
          on end, not even thinking of him. Funny,
          isn't it?

REG	You're a grown woman. It's not like you was a clumsy teenager. No reason why you should always be worrying about your Dad, wondering what he's doing, or what he's thinking.
ZITA	In his eyes I'll always be a clumsy teenager.
REG	Anyway, teenagers aren't clumsy any more. They're bloody terrifying.
ZITA	I can't imagine you being terrified.
REG	No? There's this jitty just by my place. Got them bars across to stop bikers speeding through. You know. And the bloody kids hang around out there, all bloody hours, drive you mad, twisting round on the bars, swearing and buggering about. I went out to them the other night, nearly midnight, and they just stood and looked at me, laughing. They couldn't have been more than fourteen. I mean, did their parents care where they were or what? I looked at them, and I thought, there's not a bloody thing I can do. I can't fetch 'em one, I don't know who the hell they are, and if the parents don't care then why the hell should I? And then I realised – I never know where my kids are, what they're up to. I got this creepy feeling, perhaps one of these is mine. I wouldn't have known. Four years since I saw them. They could be looking at me, laughing. I felt like the whole bloody country was full of kids with no parents and parents with no kids.

(*Pause.*)

I just looked at them for a bit then I went back in. Must've thought I was a real prat.

| ZITA | Poor Reg. |
| REG | I bet you could go out there now and bang dustbin lids together and no one would turn a hair. |

ZITA   I might do that one night ...

REG   So long as you're out there and they're safe
            inside their front rooms. Behind doors. Like
            them new flats for the elderly down the
            station – security locks and high walls. But if
            no one's actually battering their brains out, if
            we can't see them and if they're not
            screaming for help, it must be OK.

ZITA   They can be very cosy, inside they're very
            nice –

REG   Yeah? Wonder why we've got them? Need
            them? Is that nice? Is that cosy? To need
            them? Alright to end up scared to answer
            your sodding door, is it, if you got central
            heating?

ZITA   No. I didn't mean that –

REG   At the end of your life, to end up like that?
            (*He goes to the door of* SLANEY'S *room, knowing*
            SLANEY *can hear him.*) My father worked for a
            bloke like Slaney. Thirty years. Enough
            National Insurance Contributions to pay off
            the National debt. Ended up eating market
            sell-offs, cakes that started off cheap and
            then went past the sell by date.

ZITA   I know –

REG   And sterilised milk because it was a penny a
            pint cheaper. Made tea taste like shit but a
            penny a pint cheaper. Him (SLANEY) and his
            workers! (*He moves away from the door.* SLANEY
            *strains to hear what follows but can only hear the
            murmur of voices.*)

ZITA   My father never wanted things to work out
            like they have –

REG   No, but he was happy enough to hand the
            ball to you and the new lads. Too late to ask
            for it back now.

            (*Pause.*) It's how things are. That's all.

ZITA	But it shouldn't be.
REG	Get on. No good fretting. He's dead now anyway.
	Don't look so worried.
ZITA	How can you talk like that and then just shrug it off and say it's alright?
REG	It is alright. Look.
	(*Pause.*) One day you're going to worry yourself to a standstill, know that?
ZITA	I'm not that bad.
REG	No?
ZITA	No.
REG	Look at the way you're flapping around about the anniversary 'do'.
ZITA	Not flapping.
REG	Fifty thousand feet and rising.
ZITA	No!
REG	Flap flap flap. Embossed invitations. Flap flap. People arriving late. Flap. Will the champagne go round? Will the menu do? Flap flappity flap flap, flap flap.
	(ZITA *laughs*.)
ZITA	If it was just Slaney and me running it still . . . In the old days it would have been a table load of drinks, some boxes of crisps and a few sandwiches and we'd all have loved it. Now they've got a bloody Royal dropping in by helicopter. We've had to paint everything. They're bunging flowering roses everywhere the morning of the 'do' – the bushes I mean, not just the flowers. In the middle of October.
REG	Tell you what. Drop it. Say, 'Bugger em!'

ZITA   Drop it?

REG   Let some other sod worry about it all. What's
         it matter anyway?

ZITA   Well ... it was my idea.

REG   Delegate. That's what they say, your lot, isn't
         it? Go in tomorrow and say to old Tin
         Knickers–

ZITA   Miss Dodds.

REG   Say, "Oh, by the way, Tin Knickers, the
         anniversary tea party is now all yours. Don't
         let us down, will you?"

ZITA   (*giggling*) Can you imagine?

REG   (*suddenly fierce*) Don't giggle. Don't make it a
         joke.

ZITA   (*shocked*) But it is a ...

REG   No, no it's not. It's not a bloody joke. Do it.

ZITA   I can't.

REG   You can.

ZITA   It was my idea. Celebrating the day Slaney
         went public.

REG   It's nothing to celebrate.

ZITA   But it is. Of course it is.

REG   Burying the company your Dad built up, the
         workers he had, the lives they valued. Thank
         God I won't be there, that's all.

ZITA   But Reg, you'll be there –

REG   (*fiercely*) Listen. You make him go to that
         party, you smile and make him smile and
         you'll be killing him. He hates them. All of
         them. The new boys. The smart-aleck-
         moving-in-mopping-up-and-moving-on boys.

ZITA   (*trying to shrug it off*) Look –

REG	Tell them you're taking a back seat.
ZITA	But ...
REG	You know he doesn't want to go.
ZITA	I know.
REG	It's not that important, is it? Is it?
ZITA	(*eventually*) OK. I'll take a back seat. I won't ask him to go.

(*There is a moment's silence.* REG *relaxes.*)

REG	Sorry. Sometimes I think I haven't got a proper brain any more. Everything's so vague, so shifting.
ZITA	You've got a brain alright.
REG	I think sometimes there's nothing in me but the things I have to do to get by. And then I surprise myself. I feel summat. The things I was going to be. I listen to myself sometimes and I think, 'There's a nasty sod if ever there was one.' I could put you off me for life, I could.
ZITA	Please don't. Like you said, most of the organisation's done now. I'll tell Miss Dodds the rest is up to her.
REG	(*very soft, seductive*) I like you here beside me. Like this.

(*Pause.*)

ZITA	Cracker?
REG	Please.
ZITA	Butter?
REG	Mmm.

(ZITA *butters a cracker and gives it to him. She cuts a piece of cheese and offers it.*)

Half of that.

(*She cuts it again.*)

(*He slowly cups her breast with one hand.* ZITA *is suddenly very still.*)

REG   I haven't got a spare hand. You'll have to feed me. (*Very gently.*) Break a piece off.

(*She does so.*)

Feed me.

(*She puts it to his mouth.*)

Not like that. Put it in your lips.

(*Uncertainly she does so.*)

Now feed me. Like a little bird.

(*Slowly she puts her mouth to his. He takes the cheese with his mouth. She takes another, puts it to his mouth with hers, he takes it.*)

(*A third time. The feeding turns into a kiss.*)

ZITA   (*after a moment*) The crackers!

REG   Crunch crunch.

ZITA   I'm sitting on a cracker.

REG   We got a hoover. And that was a very nice.

(*She giggles again.*)

ZITA   Shush!

REG   Say that again.

ZITA   What?

REG   'Shushshshsh' like that. In my ear.

ZITA   'Shushshshs'.

(*REG roars in delight.*)

SLANEY   Zita!

(*They freeze and* ZITA *giggles.*) Zita!

(*He listens, trying to make sense of the sounds as they get up, still giggling and guilty, and sneak upstairs.*)

SLANEY   (*after a moment*) I hear them.

                  The light laugh she used to have, a man's
                  deep tones, the silence in between, the
                  footsteps on the stairs, and then ... nothing.
                  Until morning, nothing. Night after night.

                  He's made her foolish. Breathless. Flushed.
                  Girlish. (*Shouting.*) You're forty years old, for
                  God's sake!

                  (*He listens for a moment. There's no reaction from
                  upstairs.*)

                  I hear my heart, my breath, and it's all there
                  is, for me.

                  (*Shouting up at the ceiling.*) Night after bloody
                  night!

Scene Nine

*When the lights rise again it is morning. The room is untidy,
littered with wine glasses, empty bottles, take-away containers. In
his bed* SLANEY *lies listening.* REG *is half dressed, standing
central, shouting up at the ceiling.*

REG   Come on, Zee! Half eight!

                  (*He steps on something and stumbles.*)

                  Shit! (*Shouting.*) Zita!

                  (ZITA *clatters in, dishevelled and distracted.*)

ZITA   I didn't realise the time. Is there any coffee?

REG   Kettle's on.

ZITA   I'll get it at work.

REG   You've got time for a cup of coffee, for
                  Christ's sake!

ZITA   I'll be late again. She'll be looking at her
                  watch. "Good *morning*, Miss Slaney."

REG   Just remember that you're the boss. Tell her
             to get stuffed.

ZITA   Look. Give him my love. Is he awake yet?

             (REG *shrugs*.)

             Oh, Reg . . .

REG   What? The old sod's got his bottle, hasn't he?
             He doesn't need me poking me head in every
             five minutes. I'll go in in a bit. Take him out
             for an airing.

ZITA   (*tidying up*) This place is a mess. I should've
             got up earlier.

REG   Zita. (*Stopping her tidying*.) I am capable of
             clearing up a bit of mess.

ZITA   I can't help it. I relax for five minutes and it
             all falls apart. My mother wagging her finger
             'I told you so!' Getting your school things
             ready the night before and setting the
             breakfast table the night before and it has! It
             has all fallen apart!

REG   (*softly*) No one's looking. This place can be as
             much of a tip as we want. So long as we don't
             mind, there's no one else to. Is there?

ZITA   There might be . . .

REG   Who?

ZITA   Anyone. I don't know. Slaney.

REG   I won't let him in . . .

ZITA   Don't be silly.

REG   We don't have to let him in.

ZITA   (*pretending not to hear, distracted*) Oh, God,
             Reg. Look at that.

REG   Coffee. It's only coffee.

ZITA   That rug's so special, Reg, you don't
        understand. It's so – (*Shouting.*) I can't help
        it! You can sneer all you like but I like things
        kept nicely!

REG   I'll clean up. Christ's sake, Zita, I'll do the
        rug. Alright?

ZITA   I have to go. They look at me like I crawled
        out from a stone these days. And I owe it to
        Slaney –

REG   Oh, yeah, the Daddy's girl bit.

ZITA   Oh, for God's sake, get this place cleaned
        UP! (*She goes.*)

REG   (*saluting*) Workfare. Making yourself available
        for work as required.

SLANEY (*off*) Zita! Zita! ZITA! ZITA!

REG   Gone, you silly old bugger. Tip tapping off
        down the street, glad to get away from us.

SLANEY Zita!

REG   You can shout and carry on till you're blue in
        the face, but she's gone.

        (SLANEY *bangs a plate and mug together, then
        clatters a spoon inside the mug.*)

        The more you carry on the better I like it.
        Go on! Spoil yourself. Go on!

        (SLANEY *stops. He flops back, disheartened.*)

        (*quieter*) I used to comb my hair with a
        flicking motion. Like that. Wore white socks
        with black shoes. Wide boy. (*He goes to lean in
        the doorway, looking at* SLANEY.) I drove my
        fork lift with one hand. Swerving between the
        stacks. The girls stood waiting to clock out
        and pretended they weren't watching. Like
        that. (*He 'steers'.*) A silly fucking
        warehouseman in a brown overall. That's all.
        And I never realised.

SLANEY   Is that why you took this job? Did you expect her to stand watching and marvelling?

REG   I went for an interview once. Security Company. So long as you wasn't dead they took you on. No sick pay, no holidays, pay your own stamp, no pension, less than three quid an hour. I told him it wasn't a job, it was slavery without the perks. He shrugged, please yourself. So I did. They stopped my unemployment. Now whatever gets offered, I take it, see? (*Pause.*) Sometimes I think I'll tell them – shout at someone, make them listen, but you don't get past the clerks ... ah ... (*Starts tidying again.*) What's the point? There's nothing left of me anymore. Just this scruffy sod picking up empties.

SLANEY   Echoes of the past, you and me. Dead species. Extinct. They want something else now.

REG   I'll find out what it is, and then I'll be it. Do it. Go there. I can. I'm free. I can do anything. That's my strength. I hold on to that.

SLANEY   There's a lot of it around, freedom. Wives freed of husbands. Kids freed of fathers. Old people freed of whole families. Better than any war could do it, homes flattened, generations wiped out. Easy. But if it had been done by a war we'd grieve for what we'd lost. Then they'd be taken from us, now we throw them away. And call it freedom. Choice.

REG   It's the only choice some of us have got!

SLANEY   No one cares. Except you.

REG   I don't know what you're on about and I've got work to do.

(SLANEY, *tired now, watches him dully.*)

REG   Anway, why should I care what you say? If
                  you could you'd be up and out of that chair,
                  out there, doing whatever you could turn
                  your hand to, like all the other bastards.
                  Wouldn't you? (SLANEY *can't answer him.*) Lost
                  your wife. Losing your daughter. Lost your
                  work. Lost everything. You're one of us.

                  (*The lights fade.*)

                  Scene Ten

*When the lights come up again it is night time. The room is
deserted, but just as before, littered.*

*SLANEY is dragging himself painfully from his bed. He pulls
himself inch by inch across the room and into the sitting room. He
rests, catching his breath and then starts again. ZITA appears in
the doorway from outside wearing a housecoat, and puts the room
light on. She stares at him, unbelieving. He stares back,
challenging. After a moment she puts her hands under his armpits
and drags him to his chair, where she hoists him up. He helps
himself as much as he can. Breathless, she stands back while he
tries to tidy himself and regain dignity, not looking at her.*

SLANEY   Is he asleep?

ZITA   Well away. What do you want?

SLANEY   Nothing.

ZITA   You must want something. Why did you get
                  up?

SLANEY   I wanted to sit in here. On my on. For the
                  first time in weeks. He gets me up, he puts
                  me to bed. I never get to sit here on my own
                  any more.

ZITA   (*tidying up*) Do you want some tea?

SLANEY   Don't make a noise.

ZITA   He won't wake up.

SLANEY   Scared! In my own house.

ZITA	That's your fault. If you stayed where he put you, you wouldn't be scared. Anyway, there's nothing to be scared of.
SLANEY	Too late. You said that far too late. Couldn't you sleep either?
ZITA	I heard you. Slither slither.
SLANEY	How cruel he's made you. Cruel as hell. (*Pause.*) How's the works?
ZITA	(*just to hurt him*) I may sell my holding.
SLANEY	What? No!
ZITA	(*already regretting it*) I may.
SLANEY	Not without my agreement, you won't. Zita! You wouldn't.
ZITA	No. Anyway, I've not decided. It's just one option. (*Suddenly angry.*) Look, you don't know how hard it is, doing all this and running a full-time job.
SLANEY	A few weeks ago you could do it. No problem. Hand tied behind your back you could still have done it.
ZITA	Remember Mum, when you took her out? Her dark green silk suit? The way she stood at the front door, smoothing down her abdomen. Checking it was flat. Fit for the world to see. And when you came home she'd go upstairs and I'd lie in bed and watch her through the door jam, in her slice of golden light. She'd kick off her shoes and then up with her skirt, pulling faces at herself in the mirror, twisting and yanking off her girdle. And then she'd smile, all soft and blubbery and she'd have a bloody good scratch. Lovely. That's how I feel.
SLANEY	No it isn't. You have to have things just right. I know you, and this isn't you. All this mess. Look at you.

ZITA   I've just woken up.

SLANEY   Look at that table. If your mother was to see
                this now ...

ZITA   Funny, a few weeks ago I could've sworn she
                was dead, now she seems to be a reproachful
                figure forever looming threateningly on the
                doorstep. Slaney, she doesn't care about this.
                She doesn't care about fag marks on the table
                or dust on the skirting or coffee stains on the
                carpet. She has broken free. She's gone. She's
                an 'ex'. By now she may even be an 'ex-ex'.
                She's never even lived here. It isn't a part of
                her life, and neither, now, are we.

SLANEY   You've changed, more than I had thought.
                How long is it since we had a talk, without
                him? (*She shrugs.*) Divide and conquer.

ZITA   Don't be silly. You're jealous.

SLANEY   Oh, for God's sake, Zita –

ZITA   For a few brief moments every night I live up
                to someone's expectations. I like that. No
                falling short, no disappointment, And for a
                brief moment everything's alright.

SLANEY   He's killing me, Zita.

ZITA   You're better than you were.

SLANEY   He leaves me up on the hill, all morning. He
                walks away and leaves me.

ZITA   He says you're spoilt.

SLANEY   Cold baths.

ZITA   Heat dries your skin.

SLANEY   Four inches of water.

ZITA   For goodness' sake –

SLANEY   Skipped meals.

ZITA   Slaney ...

SLANEY   He laughs at me. He hates me. Zita, love, he
                laughs at me.

ZITA   I'm going to bed.

SLANEY   He laughs at you, too.

                (ZITA *falters. He immediately regrets saying it.*)

                All day long I am cold or hungry or dying
                for a pee.

                (ZITA *makes as if to go back to bed.*)

ZITA   I'll see you in the morning.

                (*Convulsively,* SLANEY *tumbles off the chair and
                starts to drag himself to the door.*)

ZITA   Where are you going?

SLANEY   Getting out of this bloody house.

ZITA   Slaney, for God's sake ... Don't be so stupid.
                Look. Please ... don't be silly. (*She drags him
                back so that he's leaning against the chair, still
                sitting on the floor.*) If you could just talk
                sensibly, tell me what's so terrible about him–

SLANEY   I've told you.

ZITA   You've got what you wanted, someone who
                doesn't dance attendance on you for a
                change–

SLANEY   He laughs at your hot rolls and your napkins.

                (ZITA *stops short.*)

SLANEY   Sneers at what he calls your 'After Eight'
                pretensions.

ZITA   No!

SLANEY   Tinned soup and a swirl of cream. Went into
                bloody hysterics. Hot rolls he said, in a
                'serviette'. He makes me crawl to the lavatory
                and pull myself up. (*Pulling himself into the
                chair.*) He's taught me how to drag myself
                around like a reptile. His great achievement.

ZITA   He laughed at my soup?

SLANEY   Christ, is that all you care about? Listen, Zita,
              he's onto a good wicket here. If we don't get
              rid soon –

ZITA   Clean linen, white cream, dainty fronds of
              parsley. A bowl of soup. Sitting opposite him,
              imagining the rings of shining cartilage, the
              silk wet tunnel. As he drank my eyes half
              closed with the pleasure of it all.

SLANEY   Zita! (*Compassionate.*) He has no appreciation–

ZITA   Oh, God. I thought I'd done it, been there
              for once, not just a shadow in an old
              photograph. He told me that when he came
              around these houses, before they were built,
              they seemed so small. Concrete slabs, divided
              by walls – mean. Individual portions. And
              suddenly that was our life, you and me.
              Afraid of saying too much, feeling too
              deeply ... I thought that with him it was all
              going to be so ... And all the time he was
              laughing.

SLANEY   No. Not all the time, love.

ZITA   It doesn't have to be all the time. It just has
              to be once.

SLANEY   I can't bear to see him any more, Zita. A dog
              lying at the side of the road with its belly
              ripped open, howling.

              (*Unseen by them,* REG *walks in and stands
              listening in the doorway.*)

              Who's done that to him?

ZITA   Please, I have to think ...

SLANEY   The jobs he's had. Lorry driving. Hospital
              portering. Swimming pool attendant. The
              man's not even forty. Nothing to call him
              back anywhere, no loyalties, no belonging.

	And if you've got nothing left to lose you'll do anything, won't you? This is just a job to him, Zita. And jobs are two a penny.

ZITA   Perhaps it was just a job. It's more than that now. He's fond of you.

SLANEY   You want him to be fond of me so, with you, he is. You want him to be . . .

ZITA   I never asked him to be anything.

SLANEY   He reads you. Anticipates. Before you know what you want he's there with it. A good servant. What sort of people have we made? Nomadic. Severed from their roots. Millions of them, swayed by any wind. Doing whatever they're told, unthinkingly.

REG   (*walking in and picking up his shoes*) We thought of marching on Poland but someone said it'd been done.

ZITA   My father couldn't sleep –

REG   What's cracking off, then?

SLANEY   It's not fair on any of us, you being here. It isn't working out.

REG   Says who?

SLANEY   Both of us. We don't have to tell him anything. We want you to go.

REG   I had gathered. When we hear voices in the night we know it's time to put us shoes on.

ZITA   Easy come, easy go, is it?

REG   All jobs are very easy come, very bloody easy go.

ZITA   You laughed at my soup.

REG   What?

ZITA   You laughed.

REG   Is that what he told you?

SLANEY	You laughed alright.
REG	Christ. You owe me wages.
ZITA	You did, then?
REG	You just told me I did.
ZITA	Slaney said. But if you didn't ...
REG	I can't be bothered, Zite.
ZITA	If he's just trying to break us up –
REG	Listen. I can't remember. Alright? I might have, I might not have. I don't keep track. I just get on with it.
ZITA	My napkins. Warm rolls.
REG	Very nice. Thank you. They were lovely, while they lasted. My Dad used to say, 'It was very nice, what there was of it – and there was plenty of it, such as it was.' But there you are. I can't be bothered, Zite.
ZITA	I thought you really wanted ...
REG	I've been trained not to fucking want. To let go. Move on. No struggle to take over the shipyard. No lock-in at the mine. All pointless. Laughable. Holding on to the cliff-face by your bleeding finger nails. Stupid bastard! You don't listen to me, do you? I've learned not to want, not to hope, not to care!
ZITA	You do care. You care for me.
REG	No! No, I don't care for you.
	(*Pause*.)
ZITA	(*stunned*) I don't believe you.
REG	(*very quiet*) Do. Please do.
ZITA	You care for him.
	(REG *is silent for a moment.*)
ZITA	You care for –

REG   Yes. I haven't perfected the technique yet.
               That's all.

ZITA   For him? You made me believe it was special,
               what I did for you –

REG   I always do what you want me to do.

ZITA   I want you to love me.

REG   Full time, is it?

               (*A long, sad moment. He shrugs, turns away.*)

REG   Every other job, I've had to have a training.
               A day or an hour or ten minutes. But I was
               qualified for this one already. He wanted a
               bastard, and they trained me for that year by
               year, job by job. (*Bright, determined.*) Right.
               That's me. No good being downcast every
               time you've been cast down, is it? Not with
               more vacancies than ever before in the job
               centres.

ZITA   I don't know how all this has happened –

REG   Don't give it another thought. Look at me,
               see? Unaffected. I live day by day, giro to
               giro, standing in the queues they put me in,
               wherever they are. Alright? Was it so
               unforgivable to laugh at your fucking soup?
               Was it?

ZITA   Yes. Yes, it was.

SLANEY   Please go.

               (REG *goes.*)

               (ZITA *stands still for a moment, crying.*)

SLANEY   He'll get something else, Zita.

ZITA   (*still crying*) Oh, yes. He'll get something else.
               (*Snaps fingers.*) Like that. I'll get this place
               sorted out in the morning, shampoo the
               carpet. The curtains could do with a wash,

see if we can get that polish back on the
table.

SLANEY   No. It's gone, that has. French polish.
Zita ...

ZITA   There's a place at Irongate. You see them
working away when you pull up at the traffic
lights. They only look like school kids. Can't
charge much. Thank God it's the weekend.
Get something sorted out. It's the anniversary
'do' tomorrow. Oh, God. What a mess I've
made of everything.

SLANEY   Think we should show our faces?

ZITA   How can we? How can I? The things I've
said to them. You have no idea. I think I
must have gone mad.

SLANEY   It'll be alright, love. We should go. Look at
them. Perky. Bright. Let off a few
champagne corks.

ZITA   You said it was nothing to celebrate.

SLANEY   I was wrong. We'll celebrate surviving.

(*After a moment* ZITA *wipes her face, goes to him
and begins to massage his neck.*)

ZITA   You're all sweaty. You need a bath.

SLANEY   I don't want a bloody bath.

ZITA   You like b—

SLANEY   I did.

(ZITA *goes off and returns with a bowl of warm
water, a flannel, soap and a towel. She puts them
down at his feet and takes his pyjama jacket off
him. She makes as if to wash his face with the wet
flannel, no soap.* SLANEY *snatches it from her and
washes himself, quickly.* ZITA *takes the flannel and
soaps it, hands it back.* SLANEY *washes his chest
and under one arm quickly, angrily. His bad arm
limits the rest.* ZITA *takes the flannel from him,*

*rinses it, re-soaps it and washes under the arm that
he couldn't reach. She rinses his chest, her
movements becoming slower.)*

SLANEY   That's alright.

ZITA   Your back. (*She goes around to it, soaps the
           flannel and starts to wash his back.*) On the
           shoulder blades, long strong hairs. There's
           something about necks. I've got a thing about
           necks. Thick strong sexy necks. Thin white
           vulnerable necks.

           (*Pause.* SLANEY *stares stolidly ahead, not looking
           at or acknowledging her.*)

           Your neck makes me want to cry, and lie
           down, and smell your skin, open
           mouthed . . .

           (*Pause*)

           Sorry.

SLANEY   I have to keep you at arm's length, Zita. I
           need to curl my arm around my head to
           ward off your love. Oh, God, what will we
           do?

ZITA   (*after a moment, calmly clearing up, cheerfully
           conversational*) You'll live your life and I'll live
           mine. Reg Dalton will live his, whatever it
           turns out to be. Wherever it turns out to be.
           And we won't disturb each other with our
           humanity. There must be a scheme for
           humanity somewhere. A small office funded
           by central government, with a tatty little
           kitchen and a sugar sprinkled tray of mucky
           mugs and tea spoons and a kettle on the
           floor. Where Reg can fill in a form and
           maybe find himself eligible, or maybe not.
           We'll go tomorrow and toast our success. The
           silver will shine. The breeze will gently billow

the marquee, our voices will be soft, and we
will smile at the Phillipino waitress. I'll tell
myself, as I break the threaded spine of a
small shrimp, that no one starves in 1990 and
that, if they did, we would find our
compassion. That everyone is alive and well
and that today's cold wine and blue sky is
justification enough for our bright short past.
That there are no millions out there,
shuffling from counter to counter with their
wide-eyed children, teaching them the
patient steps of a tribal dance. That there is
nothing to fear and nothing to grieve for, as
someone blows into a microphone, to a swell
of laughter.

That is not our fault, and that there are more
vacancies than ever before in our job centres
and they can find work if they really want it,
if they'll only be willing to move and adapt.
Let go and move on. And the smiling
waitress with the smell of the South China
Sea on her skin, will look into my eyes over
the gold rimmed plates, and turn away too
quickly, her small feet moving away silently,
dancelike.

(*The lights fade.*)